1

Taking Care of Susan:

how one woman learned to take care of herself

By

Susan Devine Napoli

Dedicated to:

Clare and Matthew

This book was written for inspiration and entertainment purposes only.

Table of Contents

5

Introduction

"Is this all there is?" I asked myself sitting at a stoplight on my way to work. I knew I couldn't live at that pace forever. I had no answer for myself. I was a superwoman of the do-everything-for-everybody kind. I was unhappy about it but didn't know what to do. This new job wasn't the answer. No answer was forthcoming. I was living a life I did not like. I got bits and pieces of something really solid; found in movies, songs, and books. I felt like I was being led. Then one day I did an ordinary thing. I turned on the Oprah Winfrey show and they were doing a series on life makeovers with Cheryl Richardson. I was riveted. My journey stepped up to a new level that day as I listened and took it all in.

This is the story of how in ordinary ways I made changes to live the life I wanted. I followed my intuition and inspiration from many sources. I collected articles, music, and movies. I read books. I made a few significant changes and many small ones. I figured out what I loved to do and did that as much as possible. I learned to slow down and do what I love more and what I didn't like less. I put myself back as the center of my life. I learned so many things about what to do to make the life I love. I meandered a lot through written materials and pastimes. I never expected it to add up to anything.

I now am in a place of contentment most of the time. I monitor myself and meet my own needs. I work. I take care of my teenagers. I write. I get pleasure from the beauty I find in each day. It is a long way from where I started. I never expected to feel this good—ever. I thought I was going to live in a distressed speeded up state the rest of my life. I convinced myself I could handle it. I learned I didn't have to handle it. Healing happened.

I wish I could tell you it was easy to do all this. I did many of the things in this book including parenting two children and working full time. I felt the foundation of my life crumble underneath me. I felt truly alone. I felt like I was falling apart. I had to make peace with the past before I could move on. I learned so much about myself. It is a daily process of centering myself to know when to go out into my world and when to retreat for a while.

The trickiest part of all of this was that there was no one in my life to guide me; not a friend or relative to call or get mentored from. I learned quickly that this was out of the ordinary to follow my heart and do and be who I needed to be. No woman in my family ever did that. She did what she was supposed to do for others. I did have some mentors in the form of authors, song writers and many others "out there". I learned that most people want their lives to be the same and the people in them to be predictable. When I made some changes I was not predictable anymore.

As you read, keep in mind that each section starts back at the beginning of my journey and the decisions that I made that took me to the present. I decided to organize it in chapters to be easy to follow and to go back and refer to. I meandered a lot gathering the best information I could find by following my heart. Then I would go out and meander some more. One day, I looked over it all and I was inspired to see what my heart had gathered and found out things about myself that I didn't know. Then I thought I needed to share it. Read and enjoy. There is much to learn from each other. I'm glad you decided to join me.

"And the day came when the risk it took to remain tight inside the bud was more painful that the risk it took to blossom." Anais Nin

My Credo

"Stop!" I said to my world. "I've had enough."

I cannot take care of you until I take care of me.

So for now, I will retreat to the sanctuary of myself.

It is there I will…
Make something,
Remember childhood,
Embrace the future,
Savor the now,
Spin magic,
Or take a nap.
And I won't come out
Until I can gain something
I can take back to my world
And it will become my prayer.

I wrote this in 1999 and hung this on my wall of my studio and nobody read it but me. I had made a promise to myself that I would take care of myself. The studio is long gone but this piece of writing lets me know where I was at the time. I still feel the power of the words.

Getting Rested

I was working full time teaching pre-kindergarten in the public school and had two children of my own under the age of three when I realized I was tired, really tired. I took my children to day care to be at the school by 7:00am. I planned my day the morning of the day I would teach it. I taught two half day classes of 22 children. At 3:30 I left as quickly as possible so as to see my infant son for a few hours before he fell asleep for the night at 6:30. I made dinner with both children clamoring for attention. After dinner I would play with them, give them a bath, read them a story, and tuck them in bed and spend time with my husband who would talk long into the night. I then woke up twice to care for my son in the night before waking to begin my day again. In the teacher's lounge one of my colleagues made a comment.

'I don't see how you do it," referring to having two children under the age of three and a fulltime job.

"A good day is when I remember to put deodorant on," I paused. "I'm not going to tell you if it is a good day." She laughed.

Truthfully, I don't know how I did it either. Part of it was I couldn't stop long enough to feel anything. I knew it was bad when my eyesight looked like it had a mirage at the bottom of what I was looking at. When I experienced this is in the morning I knew it was bad and I was going to be tired all day. I made it through the whole school year with five hours asleep a night. I got pretty rested over the summer and then I went and did it again for another year. Only this time I got a class of children in which nine of the children should not have been in the same class together. I decided to be a stay at home mom for the next few years.

I learned quickly how dull being at home with children all day could actually be without adult contact. So I got a student loan and went to graduate school earning a Master's Degree in early childhood education to have more information about working with children and to bring in more money. Although I got real interesting adult conversation I was running on empty all the time. I stayed up doing homework fooling myself I could take a nap when the children did. I actually did more homework during that time. When I graduated I started working part-time expecting to volunteer at my children's school when a full-time faculty member had a stroke and a heart attack and could no longer speak. I said yes to a temporary and then a permanent position. For the first time in my life I had homework to grade at home, while getting an oil change, and while waiting in the doctor's office. I was an expert at making myself too tired.

One day I finally decided that I needed to start sleeping more. I couldn't take the pace anymore. I noticed I felt better when I got sleep all "in one piece". I would take naps when I could. Fifteen minutes here and there. I napped when the kids took their nap. I told everyone in our household that I needed to sleep all the way through the night. I told them I was tired of leftover time to sleep. I kept getting woken up so I went into the living room to sleep on the couch. I did that for quite a while and then I found a room to lock myself in. That first night in there was heaven.

I had a lot of fantasies about going to a hotel to sleep. I planned an addition to our house to be my room. I thought about moving away all by myself. I saw a mother on the TV who was on strike. She painted a big sign that said "On Strike" and lived in her kid's tree house. The news reported on it for about a week or two and then stopped. She was not coming out of the tree house. I could relate. I felt like I was never going to get rested again. But I slept all I could. I found and article that said sleeping in one of the most spiritual thing a person can do for themselves. I would read it over and over again and take another nap.

I also started cutting back the amount of work I did at home making my day more restful. These were big goals that I broke down into smaller parts to do, or as it were, not to do. I didn't know how to begin so I decided to let the machines do the work. I imagined that the women of yesterday would want the women of today to take leisure time when the machines were running. So if I needed to do the laundry I'd load up the machine and then go sit on the couch. My family, unaccustomed to me sitting on the couch, asked me what I was doing. I told them I was doing the laundry.

A good manager delegates the work rather than doing it all themselves. As the manager of our household I delegated dishwasher loading and laundry folding. Both of these jobs nobody could do as good as I. I had a system to fit as many dishes in the dishwasher as possible and to fold the towels in a manner that fit the linen closet. But I didn't want my kids to grow up thinking only mom can do these things and I didn't want to have to be the one to do everything. My goal for them was to eventually grow up and be able to live on their own. So I relinquished these chores as I did other things. I learned to accept that clean dishes in the cabinet and clean towels in the linen closet that I didn't have to put there was a good thing.

Another thing I didn't do often was clean my children's rooms. This was their territory and I put up with their rooms looking the way they wanted them, some of the time. I did have a threshold however for the amount of mess I could tolerate. So on the day to clean I would tell my children what they had to clean and I would choose the job that had the most impact for cleaning the room and making it look better faster. Since my children wrote a lot there was lots of used paper and most of it we did not keep.

I had them clean out the paper. Then they would pick up the toys. I helped them by putting half the toys in the top of the closet and then when they tired of the toys they could reach we would switch them. This would help to eliminate the begging for the new toys when the "new" toys were in the top of the closet.

I also delegated that my husband take care of the children while I took a nap. I went into the master bedroom and shut the door. Sometimes I would get little sleep, sometimes the kids would fight and get too noisy, and sometimes we were both too tired. I learned quickly that I was getting leftover time and started scheduling myself into my own life. I realized I had to get away from it all for just a little while, a space of my own that was quiet.

With my new found money from my new job I decide to spend some of it on myself so I rented a warehouse office space in the local storage locker place. There were a few offices for rent with a large back room and a bathroom. I called it my studio. I bought furniture to do art on, art supplies to make stuff in the front room, and made a sitting room in the back room I would go there to get away from it all. As I spent time there a wave of fatigue would overtake me and sitting was not what I needed to do. Sleeping was what I needed to do. So I bought a cot and bedding and made a place in the back room to sleep. It was wonderful. I was getting more sleep and finding out how tired I really was. One day I was wishing I had a shower there too thinking I could live there and then thought against it. I started looking at apartments. I knew I needed more sleep and a new place to live would extend the amount of sleep and quiet time.

I looked at apartments and was really taken by one I saw. It was so beautiful and new with crown molding and Berber carpet. There was a resort style pool and fitness room. There was a theatre with thirty seats and a sand volleyball court. There were community activities of Saturday Breakfast, family gatherings, treats, and movie night. Although I knew there would be less money for buying things, the setting itself was a treat. With my next paycheck I would move into that apartment complex. I moved myself and my kids there while my husband was at work. In short, I left him.

I had to break away from the cycle I was in, in order to get a perspective on my life and the direction I wanted it to go. I had lost myself and needed to be able to hear myself. I needed to do what I needed to do. I couldn't wait for permission from myself or anyone else to do and be who I was. I realized I had only one life there isn't another time around. So I went to where I could be free. It was one of the most difficult decisions I have ever made and I knew it was the right one.

All moved in to my new apartment I made some rules and one of them was a mandatory quiet time at 9:00pm. At that time, my kids retreated to their room and did very quiet activity like reading before sleeping. This time was not to be interrupted. I got my quiet time too. I took long uninterrupted bubble baths, read, or wrote in my journal. I had this time every night. It was heaven. I was sleeping much better and had hours upon hours of time to figure things out. It took some time but I finally got rested.

My kids are teenagers now and they still respect the time I need to sleep. I respect theirs. In the summer and on the weekends they can sleep in. My days are much less busy then they were before. I don't take on as much. I have a rule that if they want to go out and they need me to pick them up then I need a call at 9:00pm. During that conversation we can negotiate on staying later if they get a ride from their Dad or they may get permission to sleepover at their friend's house.

Sometimes when work gets busy I can get over tired. I don't stay up late but still I get tired. One time after I had gotten rested, I was real tired and getting enough sleep. I found the book <u>Tired of Being Tired,</u> in my meanderings at the bookstore. I bought it and looked at the foods to eat. I bought some of the foods and was too tired to fix them, especially at breakfast. So I went to Jamba Juice and got a smoothie with a protein boost. I did this for four days in a row and stopped feeling so tired. Apparently, I was eating too many carbs and not enough protein. I finally had enough energy to fix the foods I bought. Since then I have learned that nuts are a quick protein I can eat in the morning with cereal and fruit.

Activities

Do laundry. Gather up the dirty clothes and start up the machine. Go sit on the couch and wait for it to go through its cycle. Listen to the water rushing in, the agitator working, the spinning, and the rinsing. Resist the urge to do something else while the machine is working. Congratulations you made it through your first quiet time. It is okay if you fall asleep.

Look over your schedule for time to nap. Determine if all the things on your list really need to be done that day. Push things to the next day. Don't do some. The earth will not end if some of these things don't get done. You know what they are. Then nap. Life is not a race to see how much everybody gets done.

Don't shoulda all over your self. Find ways to relax your mind if it races. " I shoulda been doing the dishes, I shoulda been doing this. I shoulda been doing that…" Gentle yoga, meditation, and listening to soothing music are some ways to relax yourself. When your kids grow up they will not say I liked the way you cleaned the house, Mom. They will remember the time you spent with them really tuning into them. Explain to your family you must get caught up on your sleep. If they really love you they will let you. Resources:

Greene, Bob. <u>The Best life Diet.</u> (I eat Bob's breakfasts to give me energy through the day. Even when I am too tired to exercise it gives me the edge I need when I work.)

Hanley, Jesse Lynn, MD <u>Tired of Being Tired</u> (This is a good program that shows how to get out of the adrenal rush lifestyle and adrenal burnout.)

Richardson, Cheryl. <u>Life Makeovers.</u> (This book talks about the adrenaline rush and gives things to change in your life to make it more of what you want it to be.)

Vienne, Veronique. <u>The Art of Doing Nothing.</u> (I used this book to have some ideas of what to do with the empty pockets of time I created. I gave it away as a retirement gift—she laughed so hard.)

Yee, Rodney. <u>Relaxation and Breathing for meditation</u> DVD (I did part of this DVD when I had trouble unwinding before sleep and too tired to exercise.)

Extreme self care

I must have grown up with the notion that mothers give up everything for their kids. I gave up my job for a while, my interests, my space, and my time to take care of myself. I was home taking care of my children and waking up at all hours, sleeping when I could, eating to give me energy for when I was awake, and gaining weight. I had a hard time finding room for myself in my own life. As a teacher of young children I had a profession that expected giving, and example of my own mother giving, and an upbringing that expected giving. I didn't know what size I was and each time I went to the clothing store there was more bad news about becoming another size bigger.

When my daughter was three weeks old I decided to go out by myself and do the things I did before I had her. I had to negotiate heavily for this time for myself. It was not a priority and it got cancelled and moved and changed. Back I went to negotiations until I had a regular night with a regular time and I called it Mom's Night Out. My kids never liked me going out without them. They would beg and cry and look at me with great big eyes. I told them it would make me a better mom and then I went.

I went to the dollar show for a movie, to the mall to browse through my favorite stores. One day I found a beanie baby that was in the shape of Mary Poppins. I bought it for around

$5.00 and was guilty for weeks afterwards that I had spent the money on something I really didn't need. It was like the doll I had wanted as a child but never got a store bought one. Sure, my mom made me one but a longing from childhood was satisfied that day. Later on, I found the same edition of the Boys and Girl's cookbook I had cooked from as a child at a resale bookstore for $2.00. I was getting used to and looking forward to my night out each week. I was getting used to getting things for myself that I liked.

I learned that giving myself continuous supply of small treats was very important (O magazine). It did not always mean that I bought something for myself. I started doing this when I learned to use my good stuff like my china instead of paper plates. I had a hard time using the beautiful things that I saved like candles. I had a collection of about ten small Christmas candles people had given me. I saved them for about 12 years. At Christmas when I saw them in my Christmas stuff I decided to use my good stuff and I placed them all on a footed cake plate and lit them all at once. My kids loved it. We shut off the lights and let them burn a while. Every evening we would light them again until they were all gone. I gave myself the permission to use my good stuff that day. That was the first time I remember deciding that there would be more candles. I had been so careful with the candles I had and afraid that I wouldn't get anymore. I gave up the fear that day. I didn't have the resources or more candles but I knew there would be more.

When I got the job teaching at the community college the first thing I bought to take care of myself was a terrycloth robe. I bought the best I could afford which was the middle quality robe on the rack. After I took a bubble bath I would wrap myself in that robe and sit in the living room all relaxed. My kids were little then and they too wanted to be all relaxed and snuggly feeling too. I went out and bought each of them a robe. We had many an evening wrapped in robes and watching TV.

I also read inspiring books and music. I was on the search for positive things that made me feel good because they supplied wise advice that I needed. I generally stay with nonfiction and read self-help, cookbooks, personal stories of the author and most recently, poetry. I keep only the best books that really move me and the others go to a book resale shop where I can get more books or cash. I am always on the hunt for new ideas and information. Last year I got a laptop and my son showed me how to load my music into it. I spent hours listening and loading the best and most inspiring music on to my computer. It is a different listening experience to hear only my favorite songs and music. It feels good to be soothed by music.

I subscribed to magazines. I love magazines and looked forward to finding out new things each month. I realized that the magazines had lots of things in them I was not interested in and some that were really good. So I decided to tear out the really good things that were important to me from the magazines. I would trim the edges and put them in a notebook in page protectors. Articles I collected were the wise advice that applied to me in my life at the moment. I found articles on the changes I wanted to make. I found articles on the person I wanted to become. I found articles on making room for myself in my own life. Over the years I have collected seven notebooks of articles about things that interested me very much. During my quiet time I read the articles and it would comfort me to read my favorites over and over again. It seemed the articles I really needed would come at the right time.

One thing I liked to do was to create an inviting ambiance for myself in my apartment. I would put on soothing music, soften the lighting and light a scented candle, watch the sunset, and have a cup of tea and a cookie. I would then sleep with our cat if he was willing.

I liked to go out at night and swim in the pool warmed by the sun all day. My son called it a "midnight swim". The water glows green from the lights. There haven't been many people at the pool at night lately so the water is still and I lie back on the water and look at the stars. Nature tends to be near the pool since it has tropical plants around it. Crepe myrtle trees drop pink blossoms into the water. A few times I have set a frog free from the pool. Birds congregate there, they stand on the fence and cock their eye as I swim almost silently in the water.

As I took care of myself, my thinking about myself got better. I got to know the me that got lost all those years ago. It was a very strange feeling at the beginning. I even felt anxious. I'd try to fill the silence that felt threatening to me. I played music that was gentle. I wrapped myself in a blanket and snuggled into the couch with the articles I collected and drank in the positive thoughts they conveyed. Whenever I felt I was losing my way something else would come my way; a song, a book, an article, or a television program. I did something to nurture or care for myself every day. Now I look forward to the silence and the time I care for myself. I don't do it all at once. I am gentle with myself and allow myself to go slowly. I do something for myself, however small, everyday. No day is too busy to take care of myself.

Activities

Negotiate a Mom's Night Out. It goes on the family calendar each week. It is your time to be with you. It cannot be moved or cancelled. Expect that family will not want you to go. Shut off the ringer on your phone. Trust me, they will figure it out without you for a few hours. Go wherever you want to go. Enjoy!

Magazine on my pillow. When a magazine comes in the mail I don't always have time to read it so I put it on my pillow. When I return at the end of the day there it is a treat waiting for me like somebody cares enough to leave me a treat. That is true, I really care about me. Start leaving a treat on your pillow for yourself.

Resources:

Richardson, Cheryl. <u>Life Makeovers.</u> (I got the term "extreme self care" from this book. They put it on Oprah.com in the form of little articles and checklists of thing to change and learn to take care of oneself. I printed these checklists and go back to them and check to see how I am doing from time to time.)

Ban Breathnach, Sarah. <u>Simple Abundance: A Daybook of Comfort and Joy</u> (This book has some great ideas about how to take care of yourself. I used it when I didn't know how or what to do. I still pick it up from time to time just to see the wisdom found on the page with today's date. My favorite is December 18- A birthday ritual. Try it.)

Who Am I?

Since I was about ten years old there seemed to be something different about me that I wanted to know more about. I spent about eight years confused and getting messages from kids that I was not like them. I was extremely quiet and introverted at school. The other kid's antics made me nervous. I was afraid to get in trouble. I was so quiet in student teaching that they told me I was almost too quiet to become a teacher but I did well and graduated with the warning that I was the kind of teacher some principals like to eat whole. I worked in the field eleven years with children in spite of what they said.

I had graduated from college and had had my children when I truly wanted to explore the questions I had about myself and who I am deeply. I had too many responsibilities before then to do that. On my night out I found the book the Illustrated Discovery Journal by Sarah Ban Breathnach. I was so excited to find this book. She said it was fun like paper dolls to make the collages in the book and I get to find out who I really am.

I started it and then realized it was going to be deeply personal and I finally found a quiet space with no demands which ended up being in the walk in pantry. I dragged the loveseat and my music into it. I locked myself in. I cut and pasted and started excavating the me I had lost long ago. One realization after another happened as I completed the journal. Then I came to the favorite color journal. I found I was more lost than I thought if I didn't know what my favorite color was. I was sad not to be able to remember and then found I had three: dark red, beige, and blue. That little bit of knowledge made it suddenly easier to buy clothes. I went toward my favorite colors and soon my closet was full of those colors. Then I shifted from dressy to casual and from cutesy to plain all because of the knowledge I gained from doing the journal.

I had to start saying "no" in order to get the time I needed to find out who I am. I felt swept by the sea of emotions saying yes to the things people really wanted me to do. Stopping it was not easy. I started saying no to the sales people on the telephone. Then I said no to the things I really didn't want to do. Most people got the idea quickly I wanted to do something else. Sometimes I do something I am interested in. At this point, it is a slow dribble compared to what it was before. I happened to have several people in my life that gave me problems with not being the one who would do anything for people. It took them quite some time before they moved on. Some of them still try once in a while. I still struggle with saying no sometimes. I started speaking my mind more and more. I knew I needed time to pursue the things I loved. One day it looked like I wasn't going to have the time to figure out what I loved I became so exasperated that I blurted, "Laundry is not my hobby!"

I kept a journal off and on since in 1983. At first, I remember holding back my feelings quite a bit as I wrote. Over the years I gave a little bit more until I was able to blow off a lot of steam in there about things that went wrong and record things that went good. It became a place to work out the things from when I was a child. I write often and I taught my children to write and keep journals when they were little. I bought them the really cool looking writing instruments: pens that light up, pencils with pictures on them, markers of all kinds. I made writing fun for them. I made it fun for me when I bought a journal with a leather cover and a pen set. I learned that giving myself little treats was one of the things to do for myself. I do go back and read my journals once in a while to see how far I have gone on my journey.

The biggest challenge of them all has been getting in touch with my feelings. I learned to bury my feelings at a very young age. I took a lot of time to think about my first half of life and the choices I made and the experiences I had. Pain had been stored like the proverbial elephant in the room; I always walked around it. Layer by layer I pulled back those layers and found my creativity.

For years I had been afraid to paint. I always wanted to do it but couldn't push though the fear. I would buy art supplies and would sit ready to paint and end up staring at them but I never would paint until this year. I have painted fifteen paintings and I am not afraid to paint a bad one. I'm not even sure I've even painted a good one yet. It doesn't matter. I am free enough to paint.

In Enya's song, Pilgrim. It is a song about a journey and how we are on that journey. The last three lines of the song repeat the phrase:

"Pilgrim it's a long way to find out who you are."

It alludes to the fact that the longest journey is to get to know myself. That song has both encouraged me and discouraged me. It encouraged me that I am on this journey and I can find out who I am. It discouraged me when I think that it is probably the biggest project of my life and I may not fully finish it until the last breath and even then, maybe not. I can't say what keeps me going. It's just something I have to do.

Activities

Million dollar question. When I started my journey I wanted the million dollar answer to questions like: how do I get more time for me? How do I live the life of my dreams? How will I get to know myself better? At first I had the million dollar dreams. That somehow my life would change and I would get huge amounts of time to do this. But I had a yearning so bad that all I had was twenty-five cent amounts of time to dream, to heal, and to change my life. The five minutes here and there I gave myself grew when I made one small change at a time (forgive the pun). Five minutes became fifteen minutes, fifteen minutes became a half hour…I have whole evenings to do what I love now. Look at your goal and make the twenty-five cent decision. What little thing can you stop doing to make room for something you love? Invest in yourself and watch it grow.

Resources:
Ban Breathnach, Sarah. The Illustrated Discovery Journal (out of print, see Amazon.com) (They should re-release this book it was so much fun and easy to do. It is a good tool that helped me find myself and begin to listen to myself again after getting lost and tossed around in life not really knowing what I really wanted.)

A Room of My Own

I've wanted a room of my own since I was thirteen when I saw my friend's room and realized that a person could go out and buy furniture and things to make a room beautiful and *match*. My room as a child had the necessary things but it did not match. It did not get finished. It was painted lavender (my sister's favorite color) and there were curtains on one of the two windows. My mother had made the curtains but when she ran out of thread she never got back to it. I had a white dresser, a white bed and a Kelly green vanity table. My sisters each had a wood toned bed and a dresser in the same room. I finally begged my parents for three years for a room of my own and got it when I was seventeen.

Dad is not particularly a handy guy. He is a book guy. He took me to the hardware store and he selected out 2X4's and I got to pick out paneling and paint. We got home and it wasn't long before I realized he knew how to build a wall for me to enclose the space at the top of the stairs and I wanted to help him. It wasn't long before his frustrations got the best of him and he started swearing. I left him alone and when I got back the framing of the wall was finished. I helped him hold the paneling in place and he hammered when he found he couldn't hold it and hammer. I signed my name inside the wall on the 2X4 and dated it so someone might know when we built it. Then I told him I wanted a door and he went down in the basement and got a door. He painted the walls of the room beige while I painted my furniture the same color and then I moved in. I loved it. I would sit by the hour and make stuff, listen to soft rock, and dream of falling in love.

Before I knew it, high school and then community college were over. I went away to college and then moved quite a bit. Sometimes I got a room of my own and sometimes I didn't. It is one of those things that keep eluding me. As time goes by the rooms get better and look nicer. I decorated my current apartment and coordinated everything. It is amazing how many places I have lived and carved out a niche for myself.

As the oldest of six children there was no place I could call my own for a long time. I would go outside and sit under the forsythia bushes or up in the cherry tree or the mulberry tree. I made a place in my closet more than once. Once I wanted a retreat and room of my own so bad I moved out into the garage and set up a room of my own out there. It was in the south, so winter was mild and I got an electric blanket to keep me warm and it worked. I then moved out of the house and my brother, myself, and a friend to rent a house. We all got rooms of our own in that house.

I then got married and I had a spare bedroom I kept my stuff in, like a studio. As our children were born, one by one my personal space became my children's rooms. So I went out in the backyard to the shed that we converted to a studio for me. It had everything but an air conditioner so I eventually gave it up because it was too hot and I used the garage. I made plans to convert the garage to a room but the garage would need further air conditioning that our current system couldn't handle. So I made a plan about a room on the other side of the garage. I made a plan for a garden room on the front of the house. All the plans were struck down so I got the studio at the storage offices and warehouses. And as you know, I moved into my own apartment.

Decorating my apartment was so much fun. It took me a while to do. I had learned what I liked from Christopher Lowell who encouraged his viewers to do a lot of browsing and cutting things out of the magazines that they liked. I kept the pictures in a large envelope. I watched interior decorating shows for months until I understood the basic ideas and before I bought anything. I learned an easy way of thinking about decorating from Christopher Lowell to do it in seven layers. I had decorated my previous living space. The knowledge and experience gave me confidence and I was not as overwhelmed as I was before I learned the basics. I knew my favorite colors so I bought things item by item on my new limited budget over the course of five years. I never bought furniture before so I went up the freeway going north and stopped in all the furniture stores. Then I stopped in all the furniture stores going south. I found the price range I could afford. It was in the back warehouse of a large furniture store where they had the returns and discontinued furniture. When the day came to buy furniture I went and looked at everything. I sat on the ones I liked. My kids were with me and they gave me their opinion. I chose a beige couch and loveseat with accent colors of dark red, gold, and green in the fabric. I knew when I bought it that I would buy things that went with the couch and loveseat. I chose a kitchen table and chairs in green and light wood. I chose gold colored picture frames when I lived with my husband so I brought those with me. I would go browsing often and bought things that would go with the color scheme. I bought all the items from places that offered discount prices like Target, K-Mart, Wal-Mart, and Lowe's. I would look at my living room and decide what I needed the most or I would find something I loved and buy it. Most of the time when I was out browsing, I had no agenda about what to look for and knew it when I saw that it was right. I bought what I could afford and what I loved.

Let me give you an idea of what I bought. I needed curtains so I went looking and couldn't afford them. I collected fabrics off the sale table in the fabric store. I collected fabrics of various textures and similar in color; beige gauzes, coppery wrinkled, beige lace. I cut them to length and tied the top with a string to gather it together. I took a hammer and nailed up a swag on either side of the window. I then took two more pieces of fabric and tied them together with string and hung them up across the top of the window. Then I draped the lace around the top and added long strings of pearl colored beads. I fussed with it all until the strings didn't show. I had a table that was an entry table/vanity table. I put it near the entry and the space under it looked like it needed something. I bought a large willow basket and filled it with greenery and large white silk flowers; hydrangeas and some other large white flowers. I put white mini lights in the basket to illuminate it at night. I bought mini picture frames at the dollar store and put pictures of important people in my life and the things I love. I bought throw pillows in the colors of my couch. I found a netting to put over my bed on sale for a fraction of the usual cost. When I put it together it looked good. It felt right. This was a place of my own.

The apartment I got was a two bedroom and I put both kids in the master bedroom and gave myself the other. Over time my kids got older and my daughter started begging me for a room of her own. I resisted for a long time. I looked for another apartment with three bedrooms but I couldn't give up the one I had. So I gave her my room of my own and moved my bed into the living room. Now I am at the place once again wondering when I will have a room of my own.

Time is passing quickly now and my kids are growing fast. Our cat totaled the window treatment by climbing up it as a kitten pulling it down. I noticed it had gotten quite faded by the sun. My place is showing signs of wear and updating. Soon I will begin again. I'm thinking of getting the couch reupholstered... who knows? It will be fun to go out and see what I can find. The best thing about my living space is that it is all mine. It has things that I love in it. It feels comfortable. Oprah says that "home should rise up to greet you when you enter and leave you feeling full and filled when you leave". That can only happen when the place is cared for and tended to. The residents also are cared for while they are there. The words and tone of voice that are used is positive. Each person is valued for who they are. If one person is doing all the caring they cannot feel full and filled. There needs to be the time and space for each person to retreat to that is their space where they do the things they love. Home is a place to rest, to be nourished, and be cared for. Like I did for a while, too many people are making their home a job. In my home, everybody rests, everybody has things they love to do, and everybody has time to replenish themselves. We are spontaneous about when we interact together. There is laughter and lively discussion. The chores are kept to a minimum. It is not a spotless place. People come first and that includes me. I am worth taking care of myself and nurturing myself. I do feel cared for when I leave to go to work. I look forward to coming home.

Activities

<u>Make a space of your own</u>. Look around the place where you live. What part of it does everybody who lives there know it is yours? I looked around mine and I found nothing that I didn't have to share with my family. There was no furniture that was mine, no room or space that was mine. Claim some place that is yours. It is preferable there is a door to shut out the world once in a while. How would you decorate it? Go browsing at your favorite places and buy only what you love. This can take a while.

Resources:
Lowell, Christopher. <u>Christopher Lowell's Seven Layers of Design: fearless, fabulous decorating. (</u> This book has an explanation of what I saw on his television show).

Madden, Chris Casson. <u>A Room of Her Own: women's personal spaces. </u>(This is a book full of examples of what women did with a room of their own. I designed my own spaces filling them with the things I loved because of this book.)

Organizing

As someone who moved so much (22 places in my life time) I never really got enough stuff to have too much. I lived with my husband thirteen years and over that time we accumulated a lot of stuff. When I got my job teaching at the college I realized that the space we had was too small but the space we did have was not fully being used. There were large sections of the house that nobody used because there was stuff there. So I decided to use every inch of the floor space for furniture and livable space instead of storing stuff we did not use or did not like. I decided to clear our clutter (O magazine).

At first it was overwhelming. I would get bogged down in wanting to keep everything. Then I learned that I should keep what I loved. That made it easier. I went room by room over the course of about a year or two. I went slowly and threw out a total of 44 bags of things we did not need and wasn't of use to anyone else like old clothes and 5 car trunks full of things to donate to Goodwill. I never did it when the kids were around, they wanted to keep everything. One day my daughter was enjoying some new floor space and wondered what happened. I told her I cleared the things we didn't need anymore throwing away 44 bags of stuff. She asked, "What did you throw away?" she asked. I assured her that I kept all the good stuff. That question proved to me that I did throw the right stuff out and I had succeeded in using all of our livable space.

I learned that clearing clutter was not a one time thing. More stuff keeps coming into the house and needs to be gone through and I would refine my organization. I just got better at it. Let me explain. When I moved into the apartment I put all the cooking stuff in the kitchen. To me that was organizing. Then I realized that my stuff was not where I could get at it easily. One day I pulled it all out and set it on the kitchen floor and stared at it. I was trying to come up with the categories the stuff fell into so I could place it all together and really make my kitchen work for me. Then I saw it, about half my stuff was baking stuff. I realized that I loved to bake and had purchased the stuff to bake with. So to honor that interest of mine I made a baking center in my kitchen. One of the cabinets above and below the workspace was for baking. I put specialty things like tart making pans and cookie cutters together and I group the other stuff too. Then I measured my cabinets and went out and bought containers to fit. I brought the tape measure with me and brought home the containers. I was delighted when they not only fit but contained the things I loved to bake and cook with. I went around the apartment and did that in several other areas too.

As an educator, I have several times of the year that I am on vacation: Christmas break, Spring break, and at least part of the summer. During those times I go through the closets, a depository for stuff people don't really want, and clear the clutter. I donate stuff that is usable and throw away stuff that is not. I have a few guidelines for myself to limit what I have: the Christmas stuff goes in to top of the master bedroom closet, the folded clothes go in the bathroom cabinets to be put on after bathing, and the clothes on hangers are organized by season. Here in the south we really have two seasons: hot and kind of cold. Hot weather goes on one side of the closet and kind of cold goes on the other side. Coats and jackets go by the entry door. I have one shelf of cookbooks—all healthy. The others I took to the resale shop and got cash for them. I moved the work stuff to work and the home stuff from work.

About my kid's stuff, I learned early in clearing clutter that I need to leave my kid's stuff alone. They need to be the one to go through it. I did do that when they were little and didn't know better. By the time I got to the apartment and learned better I put them in charge of their own stuff. It is very tempting to want to go in and do it but I ask them if they want help and ask them about each thing I am not sure of. Sometimes they refuse help and want to do it themselves. So most of the time it looks like teenagers live here except in the living/dining/kitchen areas.

One day I finally had enough of the look of their rooms. I wanted my living space to reflect the kind of life I wanted to live. Here is an excerpt form my journal:

Christmas Break 2008. I was inspired to organize my home and honor it in time for Christmas by Peter Walsh on Oprah and Friends on XM Radio channel 156. I had been organizing and cleaning my stuff for years. I knew how to clear clutter. Peter Walsh talked about honoring the stuff we have. To me it meant everything must have a place and be useful in that space. The space needs to work with the activity that happens there. I decided to take on my kid's rooms for Christmas. I packed up the kids and sent them to their Dad's house for five days. I even sent the cat, Dani. The week before I made the plan complete with a checklist and things I might buy. I was nervous and excited wondering if I could do it in five days, wondering if the kids would really like it. I had spent quite a bit of time listening to my kids and what they really enjoyed. My daughter even said how she wanted her room to feel (completely out of the blue, I swear). I planned to "grow up" their rooms I moved my son from boy to teenager room and my daughter from teenager to young adult. I had sensed it was time to do that. I worked like a wild woman afraid I would not get through it in time. It took a day and a half to clear the clutter and trash and rearrange the furniture. I washed bedding and went shopping for very few items. One of my goals was to use as much as I could from what I already had. As the time went by, I slowed my speed. I put finishing touches on the rooms and rested for almost two days. When the kids came in everything was ready: Christmas buffet ready, their rooms ready, and the gifts under the tree ready. They immediately loved their rooms.

I learned that I honored all of our living space. I could see a sense of relief come over my kid's faces. They now had a space where they could have friends over. These were the friends that came over anyway. They too really liked what I had done to the rooms. I was finally happy with my living space and loved living here once again. This was how I wanted my living space to look. I did feel like a lost something for a while during the five days. I took my kids out to lunch on the third day and really enjoyed it. As a result everyone felt cared for in my home. My daughter asked me the next day "How did you know I wanted it this way?" My son kept coming out of his room and hugging me. They wanted to know where we got all the new stuff. Most of my answers were, " We already had it." I learned that I needed to take vacations like this, by myself to tend to myself and give myself rest. I ate healthy and my usual cravings for sweets were gone. I lost four pounds. I felt like I balanced myself. I felt like I was on a kind of retreat. I imagined that this must be what it's like when my kids will be grown and coming over for Christmas. Even our cat Dani got a vacation to a new place. He had gotten agitated about being in the same place all the time and really loved going there. I also got a message from the universe. It went like this.

There was bag of Hershey kisses wrapped in red, green, and silver foil open on the table. I reached in and pulled out three red. The next time I went by the table I pulled out four silver. Noticing the pattern I reached in a third time and pulled out three green. I was so surprised that I set the kisses on the table and thought about it. I had been buying the candy for years and this had never happened before. What could it mean? The answer came to me that the universe can use what we have to make miracles happen. My daughter's friend said it means that I am on the right path.

Activities

Inspire them. When it is time to clear clutter again look at your own stuff and see what kind of an example you are to the people you live with. They can get inspired by the changes you are making and may want to change their space too. I discovered that clearing and working on it over time makes me feel good.

Resources:

Kingston, Karen. Clear Your Clutter with Feng Shui (I use the space clearing idea when I clean house sometimes. I am methodical starting on one side of the house and work my way around to the other side. I like the idea of treating my home as a sacred space.)

Morganstern, Julie. Organizing from the Inside Out (This book uses the idea of organizing like the kindergarten classroom putting thing in zones that match the activities that are done there. It was a small jump for me since I taught preschool for years. Why I didn't use the idea with my stuff was because I had never realized I could do that before this book.)

Nutrition and Fitness

I never had a weight problem until adulthood. As a child I wrote my bicycle as far as I could to go get penny candy. We had three acres of yard to play in. Each season had something new to see and do outside: sledding, splashing, climbing trees, running and bike riding. My mother got a family membership to the YMCA and made us go swim everyday. We went to the park and climbed and went hiking in the woods to see the "refrigerator" a large rock that the other kids said that was always cool to the touch. In order to save money we grew a garden of vegetables. We grew green beans, yellow beans, corn, squash, cucumbers, tomatoes, potatoes, cantaloupe, asparagus, beets, lettuce, peas, radishes, onions, strawberries, raspberries, cherries, rhubarb, grapes and green onions. We grew it and then put the food in the freezer or canned it for the winter. I had an organic and fit upbringing.

When I moved to Houston everything was done by car. I was working and dating and going to restaurants. Somehow I felt that I needed to eat everything on the plate at a restaurant because I ate so little. The people I was with thought I might still be hungry so I ate instead of listening to myself and how full I felt. The pounds went on. I started eating when I became overwhelmed with emotion. The emotions were hooked to both the past and the present. Two children later and two decades of doing what I wanted to do took their toll. I was 70 pounds heavier than I was twenty years before. I yo-yo dieted during that time because I didn't have enough information to do it right during and after. I got to the point where I was putting on weight and unable to take it off because I was eating too little and my energy went down which made me feel like lying on the couch. I felt real tired. Exercise was out of the question I was too tired. I started on my own and lost 20 lbs. I felt unsure about that weight loss so I finally went to Weight Watchers. I lost 56 pounds in a year. I went from a size 18 to a size 8.

I came face to face with myself. Even though I was in therapy, I didn't like to feel so transparent. I got lots of attention that I was not ready for. A few struck up conversations with me. People talked to me about their weight issues as if I had a magic key to losing weight. I was very uncomfortable with the role because I didn't know what size I was and I didn't know it would take a while for my head to catch up with my body. At Weight Watchers my leader would explain to them that the thinner people at the meeting were at the end of the program and some of them couldn't look at me.

The thing I gained the most from losing weight was the confidence that I felt in myself. I relaxed finally into more of myself even though I am not a size 8 anymore I feel good about me and taking care of myself. I'm not advocating being big. I'm not advocating being little either. I am advocating feeling good about myself no matter what my size.

In all the dieting there were some things that stuck. I always buy skim milk, not whole milk. I eat more whole grains than I used to. I drink water instead of soda—even at restaurants. I know the places and the foods that are the healthier choices. I know which foods are the higher calories foods. I grill instead of pan fry. I know that two smaller meals and one a little larger are good portion control for me. I know that I need to eat a good breakfast that includes protein. I eat off luncheon sized plates to make it look like I have more food than I do. I have glass bowls that hold one cup and ½ cup to help control serving sizes. I move when I feel restless from sitting too long. I exercise as much as I can with the time I have. When my head feels too full from taking in information I go to the fitness center or the pool when I am home. At work I walk around the little lake on a break. That is a lot of things from the apparent "failure" which I have learned and keep permanent in my lifestyle.

Getting fit is a big challenge for me. At times, I am almost sedentary. I make myself take the extra movements that I don't want to do like put away the laundry, take out the garbage, and get the mail. I have learned a little yoga from DVD's that I have. I found my head became clearer after I practiced. It even helped the stiffness I felt as a result of being in my late forties. The mind, body, spirit connection is all there in yoga. It is like medicine for me. Twenty minutes a day is all I need to feel connected to myself.

In spite of my history, I want to be fit. For quite some time, I had been thinking about an Oprah show I saw about the mom with nine children who put on exercise clothes every morning when she got up and went and exercised first thing in the morning to start her day. So I bought some exercise clothes recently and I wear them to exercise in and to go out and about in. I have gotten the weirdest looks because I am 5'3'' and a size 16/18. People my size don't wear exercise clothes. I decided that I was going to wear them anyway and behave "as if" I were fit. I also wear my swimsuit to the pool without a cover up and without a t-shirt over it in the pool. One day I will finally achieve my goal but I won't get that way unless I work out.

Activities

<u>Things to do list</u>. Make a "things to do" list that do not involve food. I found this very challenging and replaced grazing all the time with going to the library, playing with my kids, spending time at the pool and many other things. One Easter a well intended family member brought boxes and boxes of marshmallow peeps. I thought that I might eat them all and instead of getting mad, my initial reaction, I invented a game with them. Each person got a couple of boxes and separated

all the peeps. On a signal we started throwing them at each other like a snowball fight. We threw them until the peeps got flat and we got tired. There was a lot of laughter and I burned calories instead of eating them.

Resources:

Greene, Bob. The Best Life Diet
See appendix C article: "Healing Life's Traumas" (this is the research that turned me on)
See appendix C article: "Untangling yourself from the grip of addiction can seem impossible, but you can lift you to higher ground" (pp.91-95 has a sequence that is extremely gentle. I use it for when I feel too tired to do my regular practice but need to clear my mind.)

McCall, Timothy. Yoga as Medicine. (Builds the case for practicing yoga, gives yoga poses for various ailments.)

Yee, Rodney and Walden, Patricia. AM and PM Yoga for Beginners. DVD. (I do the PM yoga routine in the evening. It is real nice to do with the lights dimmed. When the routine ends the music from the menu comes on and you can stay as long as you want in relaxation pose.)

Better Homes and Garden. Family Favorites Made Lighter. (A source for having the comfort foods I love without doing so much damage nutritionally.)

Field Trips

I started taking myself out to Mom's Night Out when my daughter was three months old. It took a while before I felt relaxed enough to enjoy myself without feeling guilty. That took about a year. At first I went to the movies or the mall feeling like I missed the weight of my baby in my arms. I didn't know what to do with my hands free. I called home before and after the film and missed her the whole time wondering if she and her Dad would be okay.

As time went by I planned outings for myself to treat myself. I have been to restaurants. I started with sandwich shops and moved up to tea rooms and then to a seafood place along the seawall in Galveston. I had a shrimp dinner with a decadent triple chocolate cake. It had an ambiance of soft music, the sun setting, tidy wait staff who gave extra care in their presentation of the food. It took a while to work up to that and enjoy myself without feeling self conscious and alone.

I went into Museum of Fine Arts, Houston. I went to an art festival complete with shuttle buses. I went to the whole foods store. I sent the kids to visit their Dad and stayed home and made popcorn letting it pop all over the floor and grabbing it out of the air to eat it. I watched movies at home purchasing a goody bag of stuff like chocolates and strawberries. I got it on the way home from work and left it in the car until the kids had gone for the night then retrieved it for an evening of treats and movies. I painted with acrylic paints on stretched canvas. I watched the sunset. I walked in the rain without an umbrella. I made myself a steak dinner with all the trimmings. I went to the library and the bookstore to look everything over real good in my favorite sections. I got a hotel room by myself when I went on a convention for work. I'd spend the evening exercising then out to dinner like sushi and take a bath early and settle in to watch the Home and Garden channel. I don't have cable at home so it was double fun for me to get new ideas. I'm to the point now I can take bigger adventures and start to step out of my box again.

Activities

Just Go! Start within your comfort zone and then venture out of it. Go some place you have never been before. Be a tourist in your own town. Explore and enjoy! There is much to see and do.

Resources:

Angelou, Maya. Wouldn't Take Nothing for my Journey Now (pp. 21-24 and pp 137-139) (These two pieces encouraged me to take time away for myself and to build the life I want.)

Cameron, Julia. The Artist's Way and The Sound of Paper. (Her books encourage something she calls an "artist date" and daily walks. Try it.)

Richardson, Cheryl. <u>Life Makeover</u>. (There is something in this book that is called a "sacred day" on p.21. She called it the "sacred day" on the Oprah Winfrey Show. Try it.)

Money

As a child growing up my parents never talked about managing money. I never learned how to manage money. Dad would sit with a pile of papers and pay the bills. He made a comment once about what he called "mad money" saying when he spends it Mom gets mad. There was a family discussion about going bankrupt once and how we were to never ask for money anymore. That was when I was a teenager. That is what I went with into my adult life.

I didn't ever have all that I needed for so much of my life that I developed a yearning to have more stuff. At one point I was short $30.00 a week and couldn't get it. I bounced checks and then I got a credit card. I moved to the apartment with $9,000 of credit card debt. I couldn't say no to my children or to myself and ran it up to $17,500. I was out of control. I experience an adrenaline surge when I bought something I knew I could not afford. It felt dangerous and sneaky. It turned out the only person that it hurt was myself and my kids. I did eventually learn to say no and started paying off my bills.

I figured out it would take 56 years to pay off my credit card. Dr. Phil said not paying off your credit card is like going to the store and stealing. That got to me, he was right. I called up the credit card company. I told them I really wanted to pay it off and I didn't have 56 years left to live (I would have been 106). They lowered my interest rate from 29% to 5.5% and put my account on automatic pay from my checking account. I spent some of my retirement money on it (not a good idea) and the debt went down faster.

The lack of control stole the future fun money for the next six years and it still wasn't paid off. We haven't been on a vacation, or were able to expand my kid's ever expanding world. They haven't been out of state. It felt like being grounded. We weren't exactly staring at the four walls either. We would enjoy the amenities at the apartment complex but it stopped being so fun. The families in the apartment complex would go on vacation and my kids were left with no friends around for weeks at a time. Their friends came back with tales of where they had been and what they had done. My kids had no tales to share.

If I had the chance I would not do it again. I would never suggest to anyone to use a credit card when they know they cannot pay the balance in full every month. I have lived for seven years in fear of losing it all; my apartment and my car. There were cutbacks at work shortening my contract. I lived for 6 years with no rent insurance. The co-pay in the doctor visits increased over time as did the pharmacy. The hardest months of the year were December and August; December because of being six weeks without a paycheck and August because of the start of school supplies and clothes and elective course fees. I worried a lot. I told my kids they had to wait for the things they needed. I had to wait for the things I needed. We had to stop eating out and buying treats at the movies. We had to have free and nearly free fun.

One of our favorite family activities was "Napoli Night at the Movies". We bought or rented a movie. I bought soda, popcorn to pop, candy, and hotdogs. We would spread out a sheet (to protect the carpet) and lay out the food and watch the movie in the living room. They have loved this so much that sometimes they invite friends to our movie night.

I finally had the chance to earn some extra money and the opportunity to blow it all on something fun and keep being grounded. I decided that I would not blow it all but pay some bills. When I noticed my student loan was about to be paid off I set some rules for myself so I wouldn't continue to live this way. They were as follows:

Rule #1: Pay the bills in full. I have enough to cover my bills. There is no need for them to be late.

Rule #2; Keep a journal. Record every penny I spend. Record how I feel about it.

Rule #3: Don't give in to the kids or my wants. Focus on needs—real needs.

Rule #4: Don't give up. If I do then I will have to do it again next month to make up for the money I overspent this month.

The next morning, all the money stuff started happening. My kids wanted doughnuts the first day at 6:00am. Somebody wanted me to go on a cruise assuming I could spend $1000.00 with little notice. I was approached by a man with no money at the gas station who wanted my spare change when I had spent all I had to get the gas. Somebody else wanted me to go out of town on business and I had no money to spend and come home and get reimbursed. I was being forced to say no in a new way. I got clearer about what was truly a need and what was a want, as I went. It took about three months of this to get focused and to get my kids focused. Then the extra money started coming: Tax Return, the federal stimulus check, and the extra class to teach. I was able to pay off my computer, my student loan, my dental loan, and bring the one last credit card up to date. I was able to buy my daughter new clothes and myself some glasses. I feel like I have what I need and can't think of anything else I would want.

As of this date I have $2,000.00 worth of credit card debt and a car note. My kids will be grown before my credit card is paid in full. As I pay everything off the fear is subsiding. I feel lighter, less worried. I can meet my own needs. Paying off my debts has a unique side effect I was not expecting. I have lost three pounds. Although I am exercising and taking care of myself, it is less work that ever before.

Activities

Zero Expenses Day. When I kept a money journal one of the games that I made up for myself was to see how many days a month I could go without spending anything. I called them Zero Days. I found a lot more money to live within my means. The first month there were seven zero days. The second month there were nine zero days. Then I stopped keeping track. Join me in keeping track of how many days between paychecks you have no expenses.

Resources:

Orman, Suze. Women and Money. (I had started doing the financial organizing and decision making from reading some of her other books. I refer to it as I make the changes I need. This is good sound advice and simply put.)

Parenting

Books on parenting are plentiful. Many of them contradict each other. There are things I learned from parenting. I learned that there is something challenging and something wonderful about each and every stage of development. Two year olds get to carry the burden being called "Terrible Twos" but every age has the challenge unique to the age of the child. No stage of the child's development is adult. No stage is grown, not children of school age, not teenagers. No child should have expectations to be an adult. They are still growing and developing in their brains and bodies. They need understanding for things they cannot grasp and to be trusted in some things they can. The job of parenting is to accept the child's growing independence. From the time they say "No" for the first time to the longer and longer times away from home as teenagers they are stretching their wings and coming back to the nest for the encouragement and security only to set out into a wider and wider world.

Letting go is hard. I sit and wonder if my kids are having a good time when they go out and try something new. I let go the day they took the toys out of their rooms. I let go the day they didn't want me to kiss them good by in front of their friends. I let go the first year they didn't want me to meet their teacher the first day of school. I let go when my daughter didn't want to get ready for prom at home. I let go when my son wanted to try skateboarding. I find myself savoring the time we do have as they still live in my home.

Another job of parenting is helping children find what they are good at for a hobby or interest. Sometimes the interest grows into careers. Sometimes it is just for fun. There is no way of knowing how deeply a child will go into something. As a parent, I am concerned that saying "no" will stop and dream and kill the spirit of my child. I work within the limitations I have. Encouragement goes a long way when they express an interest. They like to feel supported by me. My daughter tells her friends about how I support her by just talking about stuff that is important to her. I don't pass much judgment on her ideas. I will remind her when the risk could create a problem and to stay with safe risks.

Safe risks involve trying something new that challenges and gets adrenaline going like skateboarding. There is inherent risk involved with respecting gravity and one's ability, not a criminal record. Safe risks involve trying new things with friends that are not illegal like going to the beach after prom and walking along the shore.

At this point in parenting I have been encouraging them to get a job and make their own dreams come true. Since my finances are limited, my kids come up with ways to expand their world and visit friends. Their friends and their families have their own versions of how to have a good time as they watch their own money.

Activities

<u>Love people where they are</u>. Every once in a while I meet somebody who discovers that children are people, real people. They are more than somebody to do things to and order around. Listen to a child today, really listen. Show interest in what they are saying. Watch them enjoy the attention and give you more. Notice what makes them an individual. Listen for the curiosity and excitement for discovering new things. Children bring life to us they are unaware of.

Resources:
Pink, Daniel. "School's Out". (This article gives alternatives to what teenagers can do that would be a better use of their time than high school.)

Gratitude and Spirituality

I had learned the lesson of gratitude earlier in my life but it got lost. Last summer I had to force myself to be grateful for what I had. I did it at the end of my yoga practice when I was in relaxation pose. I would go through the things in my mind that I was grateful for. Sometimes I would choose the same things from day to day. But as I did it I actually became grateful because I acted "as if". As if I was truly grateful. I painted a quote on my apartment wall. It says, "Each day comes bearing its gifts. Untie the ribbons." I look at it often. I am working toward a positive attitude in all areas of my life. All I have to do is remember that gratitude is nothing more than saying thank you to the universe for the good things and all things that happen to me and all that I have.

I come from a religious tradition that I practiced my whole life. But once I started dealing with the past I craved quiet like never before. So I stopped going to church and found something gentler, namely to stay home where it was quiet. It felt too intense for me to go there. I needed all the home time I could get.

I have changed to something that feels right to me. I observe nature. When I am the only one in the pool in the morning, I see the birds, sometimes butterflies. Once in a while there is a dragonfly skimming the water. I feel the water moving around me. Sometimes there are people reading and sunning themselves. The other day I rescued a little frog form the pool swimming to find a way out. He rested a long time on the deck. I feel the pulse of nature, as I call it, guiding me and leading me to be my best and most authentic. I watch the sunset and the stars come out. I watch the phases of the moon. When I marvel at the beauty of nature, it is my prayer. I have never felt so close to the universe through nature and creativity. This is what I was meant to do.

Activities

Do something that feels spiritual to you when you are closest to yourself and to your creator. Give thanks for everything good in your life. Spend some time in nature. Bring nature inside your home. Really focus on the intricacies of the natural element. Marvel at the person you are.

Resources:

Ban Breathnach, Sarah. Simple Abundance: A daybook of comfort and joy

Chodron, Pema. When Things Fall Apart: heart advice for difficult times (This is so good to read when the rough times come and hit hard.)

Everything is Coming Together

A few weeks ago things started coming together to make a bigger picture with the things I have been doing to take care of myself. My meandering has served a purpose. Every so often an idea pops into my head about what I can do with all that I have gathered. I think I am finding some balance amid all the out of control areas in my life. Here is the entry from my journal: Something extraordinary is trying to happen to me. I am bouncing back and forth between two lifestyles. It is like a tug of war in me. One trying desperately to hang on and the other is okay with whichever I choose. Here is how it goes:

Shopping for wants vs. shopping for needs

Eating sugar and sweet vs. eating whole grains and fruits and vegs.

Watching lots of TV vs. silence

Lounging all day vs. swimming and yoga

Feeling scared vs. feeling secure

Cluttered vs. cleared of clutter

Trying to please others vs. listening to myself

Living fast vs. living at my pace

Saying yes to everything vs. saying yes to things that matter to me

Yearning and wandering vs. doing what I love to do.

It's like I shift between the two. The ones on the left are holding me back and the ones on the right are freeing me to a new life. It's like the things on the left that have been an old but a not so good friend that gets me into trouble. If I focus on one thing like shopping for needs, it doesn't seem right to be eating sweets. Changing my focus in shopping from buying things I don't need to things I need has caused all the other things to line up. I feel best when I do all the things on the right. Somewhere inside a craving comes up and wants me to go to the things on the left. Then I go there and eventually yearn for what is good for me. I think a lot of it depends on if I feel scared or secure. When I am scared there is much I do to try and cover over it. When I am secure I am more present and mindful of what I do.

Years ago on oprah.com there was a woman on the message boards who was herself hurting and discouraged. She couldn't understand how lighting candles and taking baths help. I know now how to answer that. They help because this is how you say to yourself "I am worth it," worth the twenty-five dollars for the candle, worth it to spend the time noticing the flame flicker and smell the aroma filling the room, worth it to acknowledge the moment as if to say "This is my life and I celebrate it." It took me eight years of burning candles to figure that out, totaling about a dozen candles in a jar. The inspiration came slowly. I must admit I too felt longing when I first started to take care of myself. I too wanted the first five minutes of burning a candle to be like an aspirin to take away the emotional pain I was experiencing. Somehow, I kept doing the things I love to do as I was inspired to do them.

I am at the point now where taking care of myself is a way of life. I follow my heart more and more. Today I am on a "stay-cation" at home from work for the holiday. I decided to do only what seemed right to do at the moment for the day. I do this from time to time sometimes for only and hour or two, sometimes for the day. I usually write in my journal, prepare something to eat when I am hungry, go swimming, watch TV, and lounge around reading magazines. I do not look at the time just move from one thing to the next when it feels time to do something else. It took me a long time to be able to do this without feeling guilty. Now, it feels wonderful and peaceful.

There are new things around the corner that I could only guess at, at this point. I feel good and starting to do new things like writing the proposal for this book. My hope is that you find the courage to reach just a little everyday and grow. Perhaps your meanderings will take you to new places. I truly never expected it to do that for me and now I have this book ready to go out into the world. I can't wait to see where it goes.

"Listen to yourself and then you will know what to do"

I heard the quote for the first time and had no idea how to listen to myself. I was sure I could do it if I only knew what it was. This was a perplexing quote for me so I decided that I would find out. I read a lot of books. I had never really taken the time to really hear myself I was always so busy. I found in my slowed down life I had time to figure it out.

January 13, 2007: The day I heard myself for the first time

Appendix A: the books I read on my journey

These are the books that I read on my journey:

Anderson, Joan. <u>A Weekend to Change Your Life</u>

Angelou, Maya. <u>Wouldn't Take Nothing for my Journey Now</u> (pp. 21-24 and pp 137-139)

Ban Breathnach, Sarah. <u>Simple Abundance</u>: <u>A daybook of comfort and joy</u>

Ban Breathnach, Sarah. <u>The Illustrated Discovery Journal</u> (out of print, see Amazon.com)

Ban Breathnach, Sarah. <u>Something More</u>

Beck, Martha. <u>Steering by Starlight: Finding your right life no matter what</u>

Better Homes and Garden. <u>Family Favorites Made Lighter.</u>

Bender, Sue. <u>Everyday Sacred: a woman's journey home</u>

Bosak, Susan V. <u>Dream: a tale of wonder, wisdom & wishes</u>.

Byrne, Rhonda. <u>The Secret</u>

Canfield, Jack. <u>The Success Principles</u>

Cameron, Julia. <u>The Artist's Way</u>

Cameron, Julia. <u>The Sound of Paper</u>

Cameron, Julia. <u>Walking in the World</u>

Chodron, Pema. <u>When Things Fall Apart: heart advice for difficult times</u>

Dillard, Annie. <u>Give it All Give it Now: one of the few things I know about writing</u>

Greene, Bob. <u>The Best Life Diet</u>

Hanley, Jesse Lynn, MD <u>Tired of Being Tired</u>

Kingston, Karen. <u>Clear Your Clutter with Feng Shui</u>

Lindberg, Ann Morrow. <u>Treasures from the Sea</u>

Lowell, Christopher. <u>Christopher Lowell's Seven Layers of Design: fearless, fabulous, decorating</u>

Madden, Chris Casson. <u>A Room of Her Own: women's personal spaces.</u>

McCall, Timothy. <u>Yoga as Medicine: The yogic prescription for health and healing</u>

Morganstern, Julie. <u>Organizing from the Inside Out</u>

Murray, Elizabeth. <u>Cultivating Sacred Space: Gardening for the soul</u>

Paush, Randy. <u>The Last Lecture</u>

Pink, Daniel. <u>The Whole Mind: how right-brainers will rule the world</u>

Richardson, Cheryl. <u>Life Makeover</u>

Richardson, Cheryl. <u>The Art of Extreme Self-Care</u>

Sher, Barbara. <u>It's Only Too Late if You Don't Start Now</u>

Silverstein, Shel. <u>The Missing Piece</u>

Silverstein, Shel. <u>The Missing Piece Meets the Big O</u>

Somerset Studio. (Magazine) <u>Where Women Create.</u> Inspiring work spaces for extraordinary women.

Vanzant, Iyanla. <u>Living Through the Meantime</u>.

Vienne, Veronique. <u>The Art of Doing Nothing.</u>

Vienne, Veronique. The Art of Imperfection.

Winfrey, Oprah. The Oprah Winfrey Show 20th anniversary collection DVD set
                Disc 1: Heartprints, Disc 2: Home, Disc 5: Books, Angels

Winfrey, Oprah. O magazine and O at Home.

Yee, Rodney. Relaxation and Breathing for meditation DVD www.gaiam.com

Yee, Rodney and Walden, Patricia. AM and PM Yoga for Beginners. DVD

Appendix B: What I did to take care of myself

Write a credo.

Blow bubbles: I have a perfume bottle style with a mini wand. It makes bubbles the size of blueberries.

Indulge in bubble baths

Watch candles burn, enjoy my favorite scent

Throw a birthday party for myself: see Simple Abundance December 17 entry. I did this in addition to the things my family did for me. I appreciated their gifts more when I took care of myself.

Rent a movie, buy Lindt Lindor Truffles milk chocolates (red wrapper) and strawberries

Eat a brownie with nuts and frosting

Eat Pepperidge farm cookies: brownie cookies and the holiday cookies with the peppermint pieces on the back. These are worth hiding.

Drink English Breakfast Tea

Get some smooth stones and a permanent marker. Write encouraging words on them.

Paint on canvas with acrylic paints and play favorite music while painting.

Make a collage.

Put a sign on the door of the room of my own that says: a woman needs a place to nurture herself.

Collect quotes.

Go for a walk in the neighborhood or at the mall with the mall walkers.

Nap with a pet.

Buy lots of pillows for my bed.

Get a small lamp to attach to the wall to make a reading spot.

Put up white mini lights and turn out the lights.

Put white rope lights around the perimeter of a room on the floor.

Roll up white towels in the bathroom, hotel style.

Make comfort food: There are lots of cookbooks that have recipes of comfort foods. I found one that reduced the calories of comfort foods.

Buy my favorite toy that I had as a child.

Pop popcorn on the stove and leave the lid off. Allow some of it to pop all over the floor. Watch out for the oil spatters.

Buy flowers for yourself. Put them in a place to see them often.

Wrap in a warm blanket straight out of the dryer.

Get small picture frames and place in them my favorite people, things I love to do, and or quotes. I got mine at the dollar store.

Organize photographs into albums.

Watch the butterflies.

Watch the bats come out at dusk.

Watch the sunset.

Try yoga.

Sit in a Jacuzzi tub until you float off the seat.

Watch the antics of my pet and my kids.

Sit and "do the laundry" by letting the machine do the work.

Shut off the TV and enjoy the silence. (This one takes a while if you are used to the TV or radio playing. Silence feels good.)

Take a day and hide all the clocks. (Eat when you feel hungry. Sleep when you feel tired. Do what you feel you need to do to nurture yourself.)

Drop off clutter to the Goodwill knowing I am helping someone else.

I went to wallwords.com and chose a favorite quote to put up on my wall to encourage myself.

Lay back and watch the clouds.

Walk in the rain with no umbrella. In the Houston area the pavement gets hot and the water gets warmed, feels good to walk in.

Eat a frozen treat. My favorite is the Skinny Cow ice cream sandwiches.

Make warm cider in the winter using Mulling Spices found at Williams-Sonoma.

Have a cup of hot chocolate after the kids go to sleep.

Enjoy my comfort food combination: Grilled cheese, dill pickle, and hot chocolate.

Make my favorite cookies: chocolate chip, oatmeal, and peanut butter.

Write in my journal.

Keep an <u>Illustrated Discovery Journal.</u>

Play sunrise music as I watch the sunrise.

Go to a ready made food bar in the grocery store and treat myself to a meal that I wouldn't ordinarily eat. I go to Whole Foods or HEB to get the food.

Sing with the radio in the car.

Soak my feet.

Sip fresh lemonade.

Make a vision board of things I want in my life.

Go feed the ducks at a pond.

Go to the community garden and enjoy the foliage and flowers.

Go outside and get some sun.

Allow myself to dream big.

Appendix C: Favorite Articles

"The Journey" O, The Oprah Magazine, July 2001, pp 31-33.

"Growing Wings" O, The Oprah Magazine, January 2004, pp140-141,

"I Love You Just the Way You Were" O, The Oprah Magazine, May 2005, pp193-194,

"The way of the Tender Heart" O, The Oprah Magazine, October 2001, pp166-168

"She's Come Undone" O, The Oprah Magazine, September 2004, pp 302-305, 327-330

"Healing Life's Traumas" Yoga Journal, June 2007, pp 41-44

"Untangling yourself from the grip of addiction can seem impossible, but you can lift you to higher ground" (This has a very gentle yoga sequence.)Yoga Journal, September 2008

"I think I'll be Lazy" Weekend magazine, p.144

"unknown" O, The Oprah Magazine, December 2000, pp186-188

"A Room of One's Own" Victoria magazine, pp 54-57

"How to Make a House a Home" Family Circle, 2/15/2000, pp 72-77.

"The Weary Women's Manifesto" O, the Oprah Magazine, July 2003, pp 144-145, 182

Appendix D: Favorite Music

A Walk in the Forest "Cavatina", "Your Warm Shaded Forrest", "Afro-Cuban lullaby"

Rascal Flatts, Me and my Gang "My Wish"

Mariah Carey, Charm Bracelet "Through the Rain"

Enya, A Day Without Rain "Pilgrim"

Enya, Amarantine "Long, Long Journey"

Dion, Celine and Andre Bocelli, These Are Special Times, "The Prayer"

Appendix E: The Places I Went

Barnes & Noble

Border's Books

Half-Priced Books

Baybrook Mall

Mall of the Mainland

Lowe's

Museum of Fine Arts, Houston

Ikea

Wal-Mart

Target

K-Mart

Dollar Movie

Dollar General Store

AMC Movies 30

Laura's Tea Room

Subway

Mc Donald's

Taco Cabana

Landry's

Freeman Branch Library

Whole Foods

Central Market

Walgreen's

Pizza Hut

La Quinta Hotel

Charleston Tea Room

Old Towne Spring

Natural Science Museum—Butterfly Exhibit

Jamba Juice

Appendix F: the program

This is for those that want a plan to follow. It is the things that I did in a simple plan. It can help you to get started as you find your own way to your own path. It does take a while to find the path and to decide what you want in your life.

1) Get rested. Do whatever it takes to get eight hours of sleep a night.

2) Start a Mom's Night Out. Schedule it in to your weekly schedule. This is non-negotiable. Don't do errands. Don't see friends. Spend time by yourself with you.

3) Get a room of your own, This is the place you can retreat to. The men got the garage and or the den. This is a female version. Decorate it all yourself for yourself. Nobody goes in there but you. Decide what you want to do in there and fill it with your favorite stuff. Let your family know that this is your space and if they want something they have to knock. Then go out and meet their needs.

4) Decide what you need to do next. Choose from the following:
   - clear clutter
   - organize your home
   - meet your nutrition and fitness needs
   - go on field trips

- get some money of your own, in your own name
- find out how to parent better until your home is calm for portions of the day
- be grateful and meet your spiritual needs

5) Do the above things that apply to you.
6) Give yourself all the time you need. Make no goal dates.
7) Keep going until you hear your own inner voice. Then you will know what to do.

Acknowledgements

Special thanks to authors who mentored me through their books: Maya Angelou, Sarah Ban Breathnach, Julia Cameron, Cheryl Richardson, Pema Chodron, Bob Greene, Ann Morrow Lindberg, Chris Casson Madden, Timothy McCall MD, Barbara Sher, Suze Orman, and Julie Morganstern.

Thanks to the radio and television shows that nurtured me and gave me hope for something better: Extreme Makeover: Home Edition, Christopher Lowell Show, Oprah Winfrey Show, Joel Osteen, Houston PBS, and Oprah and Friends XM Radio channel 156.

Thanks to those who mentored me through magazine articles: O the Oprah magazine, O at Home, and Yoga Journal. Thanks to Martha Beck for her column in O magazine, I look forward to it every month.

Thanks to the professionals who guided me through: Beth Fowler, Ed. D., Aileen Oandasan, MD, Jan J Poage, MD and Naomi Rosborough, MA.

Susan Devine Napoli lives with her two kids and two cats in Houston, Texas.